1,000,000 Books

are available to read at

www.ForgottenBooks.com

Read online
Download PDF
Purchase in print

ISBN 978-0-260-38114-9
PIBN 11181603

This book is a reproduction of an important historical work. Forgotten Books uses
state-of-the-art technology to digitally reconstruct the work, preserving the original format
whilst repairing imperfections present in the aged copy. In rare cases, an imperfection in
the original, such as a blemish or missing page, may be replicated in our edition. We do,
however, repair the vast majority of imperfections successfully; any imperfections that
remain are intentionally left to preserve the state of such historical works.

1 MONTH OF
FREE
READING

at

www.ForgottenBooks.com

English
Français
Deutsche
Italiano
Español
Português

www.forgottenbooks.com

Mythology Photography **Fiction**
Fishing Christianity **Art** Cooking
Essays Buddhism Freemasonry
Medicine **Biology** Music **Ancient
Egypt** Evolution Carpentry Physics
Dance Geology **Mathematics** Fitness
Shakespeare **Folklore** Yoga Marketing
Confidence Immortality Biographies
Poetry **Psychology** Witchcraft
Electronics Chemistry History **Law**
Accounting **Philosophy** Anthropology
Alchemy Drama Quantum Mechanics
Atheism Sexual Health **Ancient History**
Entrepreneurship Languages Sport
Paleontology Needlework Islam
Metaphysics Investment Archaeology
Parenting Statistics Criminology
Motivational

JERUSALEM

BY

JOHN L. STODDARD

Illustrated and Embellished with One Hundred
and Twenty-one Reproductions
of Photographs

JERUSALEM

BY

JOHN L. STODDARD

ILLUSTRATED AND EMBELLISHED WITH ONE HUNDRED
AND TWENTY-ONE REPRODUCTIONS
OF PHOTOGRAPHS

CHICAGO
BELFORD, MIDDLEBROOK & COMPANY
MDCCCXCVII

JERUSALEM

JERUSALEM

PALESTINE has an area only a little larger than the State of Massachusetts, while Russia occupies one-seventh of the habitable globe; yet in the scales of intellectual and moral value the little province of Judæa outweighs beyond comparison the empire of the Czar. There was a time when, even from a material point of view, Syria could not be despised. Rome counted it her richest province. One of the choicest gifts which Antony bestowed on Cleopatra was the magnificent Palm Grove on the plain of Jericho, of which at present not a trace remains. Even

RUINS OF CAPERNAUM.

to-day, with proper irrigation, some districts of the Holy
Land could offer to the Syrian sun as splendid fields of grain
as ever fringed the Nile with green and gold. But man's
envy of the beauty and fertility of Palestine produced its ruin.

Lying midway between Assyria and Egypt, and bordered
on the east by deserts swarming with nomadic warriors, this

JAFFA.

land has lain for ages like a beautiful slave in the market-
place, contended for by wrangling rivals. All the great
powers of antiquity, Assyria, Persia, Greece, Rome, Egypt,
and Arabia, have in turn possessed it; and billows of destructive conquest have rolled over it like tidal-waves, wrecking its
architectural glories, and sweeping much of its historic
splendor into oblivion.

Association with the past, therefore, is everything in Palestine. Without that charm, of all the countries in the world
it is perhaps the least attractive. But invoke the aid of mem-

ory and imagination here, and its once fertile plains will be adorned with splendid cities, while over its historic landscapes will be hung a veil of romance. Summon from its hills the echoes of the past, and every stone will seem a monument and every ruined wall a page of history.

The usual approach to Palestine, it must be said, is not romantic. It was early in the morning when the steamer which had brought us from Port Saïd, in Egypt, halted before that celebrated seaport of the Holy Land,— now called Jaffa, but known in ancient times as Joppa. The city rises almost perpendicularly from the sea, and if that sea be rough, no traveler will forget his landing there; for, although one of the oldest cities in the world, Jaffa has as yet no harbor, and half a mile from shore, passengers are lowered from the steamer into little boats, manned by gesticulating, howling natives. These boats are then with difficulty guided through a semi-circular belt of rocks, some of which lift their savage tusks above the waves, while others lurk below the surface, ready to tear the keel from any vessel that encounters them. To one of these rocks, according to mythology, Andromeda was chained, until released by her deliverer, Perseus.

We found the surf which beat upon these reefs even more violent than our boatmen. There was continual danger of capsizing,—a fate which, just at this particular place, appeared

especially uninviting, since here it was that Jonah, when ejected from the ship, is said to have been swallowed by the whale. The previous stormy night, however, had so

MARKET-PLACE — JAFFA.

appealed to — everything within us — that we gladly ran all risks, and even Jonah's brief seclusion in the *camera obscura* he was forced to occupy, seemed not much worse than what we had endured while in our little state-rooms.

At last the ordeal was over, and we found ourselves—a trifle pale from our exciting advent through the breakers— within a market-place abounding in all kinds of fish and fruits, including the unrivaled "Jaffa Oranges." Among the traders' booths and a variety of primitive vehicles moved representatives of half a dozen different nationalities. Never again shall I be heartless enough to say of my worst enemy— "I wish he were in Joppa." Life is too short for such severity. I still recall that walk to our hotel, when, hollow-hearted from a night of sea-sickness, and moist and mucilaginous from the spray that had dashed over us in the boats, we picked our way through mud and filth, now dodging to avoid a donkey, now almost rubbing noses with a camel, and ever and anon inhaling odors which proved that, even in this land of sanctity, "cleanliness is" *not* always " next to godliness."

It was in Joppa that Dorcas lived, the good woman who was so skilful with her needle; but judging from the ragged clothing of the people here, she has had no successors. It would be hard to find a place where Dorcas Societies are more needed than in Jaffa.

Nor were the faces that we saw around us calculated to command either our confidence or admiration. Two men who were grinding corn between flat stones looked more like anthropoid apes than human beings. One appeared decidedly sad, the other jovial, like the familiar portraits of babies "before and after using Pitcher's Castoria." The first possessed a face as thickly lined with wrinkles as a piece of corrugated iron, and we felt sure that in a storm the rain must run in regular channels down his cheeks; while his companion's countenance wore a smile which cut his features into two black hemispheres, leaving his curly beard to wag beneath his chin like a small shopping-bag of Astrachan fur. Two other characteristic specimens of humanity were lounging on the steps of the "Twelve Tribes' Hotel." One was a Greek, the other

(several shades darker in complexion) was an Arab. Both were so fancifully dressed, that a newcomer might suppose them to be singers in a comic opera. Put Francis

SAD AND JOVIAL.

Wilson in the streets of Jaffa, wearing his make-up as the "Merry Monarch," or the "Oolah," and he would seem to a tourist just landed there a sight no stranger than most

CEDAR OF LEBANON.

of the eight thousand souls that constitute the population of this Syrian seaport.

Yet the historical associations of Jaffa render it worthy of respectful interest. For ages it has been the ocean-gateway to Jerusalem. To its portals, in King Solomon's time, was brought the wealth of Tyre and Sidon; and on the very waves through which our boats had struggled to the land, floated, three thousand years ago, the famous cedars of Mount Lebanon, sent by a Syrian monarch for the Hebrew temple. Jaffa has been possessed successively by Jews, Phœnicians, Romans, Moslems, and Crusaders, and even the first Napoleon left here dark traces of his path of conquest; while, century after century, pilgrims from every quarter of the globe have made their way through this old war-scathed city toward the Holy Sepulchre.

The place in Jaffa most visited by these pilgrims is the reputed house of Simon the Tanner. There are, it is true, two other houses which dispute this claim, but this, for some cause, is the one exhibited by the guides, and thus a handsome revenue rewards its owner; for, when properly recompensed, he graciously conducts all visitors to the flat roof on which Saint Peter is alleged to have had that dream which warned

WOMAN IN JAFFA.

A THREE-HORSE COACH.

him to regard no people as unclean, but to proclaim his message of good tidings to the world at large, —not merely to the Jew, but also to the Gentile. There is, of course, little probability that this is really the house where Peter lodged nineteen centuries ago, though possibly the original was quite as unpretentious as the present structure. Yet, as a characteristic Oriental dwelling, it calls to mind the fact that on just such a roof as this, certainly in this very town, a humble fisherman of Galilee learned the great lesson of the brotherhood of man, which, when proclaimed, was so to revolutionize the world, that now, within the city of the Cæsars, the most magnificent temple of Christian-

HOUSE OF SIMON THE TANNER.

ity, St. Peter's, bears his name. Until within the last few
years, saddle-horses, or else a lumbering three-horse coach,
afforded the only means of transportation from Jaffa to
Jerusalem, along a highway fairly passable for vehicles. But
now a railroad has been built over this distance of thirty-
three miles, and once a day the iron horse draws tourists
across the plains of Sharon; a railway bridge surmounts the
brook where David chose the smooth stones for his combat

RAMLEH.

with Goliath; a lo-
comotive's whistle
wakes the echoes
of Mount Zion;
and the conductor
might with reason
call out to his pas-
sengers, en route,
"Ramleh,—re-
puted residence of
Nicodemus and Jo-
seph of Arimathea,
—five minutes for
refreshments." At
the time of our
visit, however,
steam-cars had not yet made their appearance in the land
of Abraham. Accordingly our party made the journey on
horseback.

After one leaves the fertile environs of Jaffa, the land
grows desolate and sterile. Even the celebrated Plain of
Sharon is but the shadow of its former self, for its whole
extent was once cultivated and well watered, and teemed with
a contented, prosperous population. The hills between this
and Mount Zion are extremely barren. The rocks reflect the
sun with angry glare, and only a few trees remind us of the

splendid forests that once flourished here. Along the road are many ruined watch-towers resembling heaps of bones gnawed and abandoned by the dogs of time. Once they were needful; for until recently this customary path for Christian pilgrims was a resort for bandits. In fact, a little town

A CHARACTERISTIC RUIN.

between Jerusalem and Jaffa is still called after the most famous of Syrian robbers, who, with six brothers and nearly a hundred formidable henchmen, was for a score of years the terror of the community.

In the number of its desolate ruins Palestine takes precedence even of the country of the Nile. Hardly a hill-top rises in Judæa which is not strewn with vestiges of fortresses or cities of a former age, reminding us of constant warfare during successive centuries.   Accordingly, the secular associations of the Holy Land at first overshadow its sacred ones.

THE OLD WALLS.

That these gray rocks had echoed to the shouts of Roman legions, conquering Arabs, and the steel-clad warriors of the Cross, seemed to us perfectly credible.   But the Jerusalem of our childhood—the Judæa of the Bible—appeared at the outset as distant from us here as when we had looked forward to this tour four thousand miles away.

When, therefore, our old guide informed us that from the next hill we should see Jerusalem, I looked at him incredulously.   Then, suddenly, I felt a quick bound of my heart, and, spurring my horse on to his utmost speed, I galloped furiously to the summit.   Jerusalem at last!

The view of the Holy City as one approaches it from Jaffa, is not so broad and comprehensive as from other points, but the first glimpse of its historic walls from any point can never be forgotten.   No spot on earth appeals so powerfully both to the intellect and the emotions.   No equal area of our globe has been the theatre of events which have so influenced the history of mankind.   It is the city of Abraham, of David, of Solomon, and of Jesus; the city, too, of Titus and of

Tancred. In one great flood of emotion the old religious memories of early years swept over me, until the walls and towers grew blurred and indistinct, and I could understand the feelings of the old Crusaders, when they first saw this City of the Cross, and amid solemn prayers, exultant shouts and sacred song, each knee sank trembling in the dust, and mailed warriors from distant lands clasped hands and wept for joy.

Alas! if only we could always feel those first emotions which the distant vision of Jerusalem excites! But, as is the case in almost every Oriental town, the shock which one encounters on a close approach is disenchanting. It is true, its massive towers are quite in keeping with our historical reminiscences, and Arabic inscriptions on the Moorish gate recall the conquest of the city by the Caliph Omar. But swarms of pilgrims, traders, and repulsive beggars instantly surround us, amidst a crowd of horses, donkeys, dogs and camels,—

THE JAFFA GATE.

and if we lift our eyes to heaven for relief, we see on one of the sacred walls the *fin de siècle* legend: "Cook's Tourist Office, inside Jaffa Gate." One naturally laughs at this,

because it seems as if there were now no spot on earth
exempt from "personally conducted parties." But let us
do this justice to the name thus displayed on the walls of
Zion: If there be any part of the world where management
like that of this experienced cicerone is needed, Palestine is
the place.   Here, where practically no traveling conve-
niences existed twenty-five years ago, arrangements have
been so perfected, that one can now journey through Judæa

in comparative
luxury as well as
safety. We trav-
eled in no "per-
sonally conduct-
ed" party, but
we did avail our-
selves gladly of
the system intro-
duced here by
that friend of
travelers, and,
while perfectly
independent in
our plans, were
fitted out with a

THE JAFFA GATE (FROM WITHIN).

reliable guide, tents, bedding, rugs, mules, horses, five ser-
vants and an excellent cook;—all so excellent indeed, that,
when outside the city in our tents, we fared much better
than in a Jerusalem hotel.   These comforts and attendance,
it may be said, we obtained at an individual cost of about
six dollars a day.

    The first thing we accomplished on the morning after our
arrival in the Holy City, was to make the circuit of Jerusalem outside its belt of stone.   It is a short excursion, for
the area of the Holy City is small.   The wall inclosing it is

only two and a half miles long, and one can easily walk round the city in an hour. Even in ancient times, although relieved by suburbs, Jerusalem must have been exceedingly compact, and at the period of the Hebrew festivals doubtless was thronged with people. Small though it be, however, a line of fortifications has environed it from the earliest times. History and poetry alike frequently refer to this,

AROUND THE WALLS.

as in the Hebrew poet's exultant ode: "Walk about Zion. Go round about **her**. Count the towers thereof. Mark well her bulwarks."

Nor does it seem strange to find the Holy City fortified. Its situation naturally makes of it a fortress. Jerusalem is emphatically a city set upon a hill. It has an altitude of

ANCIENT JERUSALEM.

twenty-six hundred feet above the sea. Built on a natural bluff, three sides of it look down on deep ravines which take the place of moats, and would, if filled with water, make the city a peninsula. Had it possessed a valley on the fourth side also, Jerusalem would have been impregnable to ancient modes of warfare. The present walls, which were built by the Sultan Suleiman in 1542, are of course almost worthless now; for one hour's bombardment with modern cannon would make them fall as flat as those of Jericho. Yet, from a distance, Jerusalem still presents the appearance of a fortress; for these old battlements are nearly forty feet in height, and are marked at intervals by projecting towers. Of these the most remarkable, alike for antiquity and strength, is the Tower of David, which was the last point in Jerusalem to yield when the city was captured by the Crusaders; and when the other turrets were destroyed by the Moslems in the thirteenth century, this admirable specimen of mural masonry was spared.

The handsomest of the portals which pierce the walls encircling Jerusalem is the Damascus Gate. It is comparatively modern, as one sees it now, having been built by a Mohammedan caliph about three hundred years ago, but excavations prove that its foundations are of great antiquity. Hence we may lose ourselves in endless speculations as to the famous men who from this point have gone forth from Jerusalem to leave their record on the page of history. Thus,

DAMASCUS GATE.

beneath the arch which no doubt rested on these same foundations, Paul may have set forth on his tour of persecution, "breathing out threatenings and slaughter" toward all

Christians in the north, though destined subsequently, in Damascus, to become a convert to, and the most powerful defender of, the Christian faith. It is positively known, too, that through the Damascus gate, in the year 1099, the brave crusader, Tancred, and his followers made their victorious entry into the city.

In one part of the wall, some thirty feet above the ground, we saw, projecting from the masonry, a small round column which bore a grotesque resemblance to a peg on which a giant might have hung his hat. The Moslems have a tradition that Mohammed will seat himself on this column at the Day of Judgment, to decide the fate of all the people who will then be gathered in the vale below. Why he should choose to sit astride this uncomfortable shaft, instead of occupying a chair on the top of the broad wall, it is difficult to conjecture. Here tradition, nevertheless, assigns his seat, and from this point, it is affirmed, there will be stretched across the intervening valley to the Mount of Olives a bridge as narrow as the blade of a Damascus sword, upon which every one must walk as the decisive test of orthodoxy. It is expected that the followers of the Prophet will glide along this elevated road as safely as an acrobat; but that all others

THE GOLDEN GATE AND MOSLEM GRAVES.

OLIVE GROVE.

will fall into the valley yawning to receive them, and thence will be transported to perdition!

Aside from such absurdities, however, the thoughts suggested by the belt of masonry which surrounds Jerusalem are most impressive. Transfigured by the lurid light of its eventful history, the name Jerusalem, or the "City of Peace," might seem to have been given to it in irony. Of all the cities in the world, Jerusalem is the least entitled to this appellation. The "City of Sieges" would be a more appropriate title, for it is one of the distinctive facts about Jerusalem that it has sustained more terrible and destructive sieges than

MOHAMMED'S SEAT.

any city upon earth. It withstood for months many of the finest armies of antiquity; and, when compelled to yield, the pertinacity and valor of its defenders were punished by an amount of cruelty and bloodshed unsurpassed in history. How strange, then, that this Hebrew capital, so deeply

WHERE STEPHEN WAS STONED

LEPERS.

stained with blood, should have acquired universal interest, not through some mighty king or warrior, but through the "Prince of Peace"—an un-resisting, uncomplaining martyr, who, somewhere on this very hill, besought His Father to forgive His murderers, and gave a memorable lesson in humility by washing His disciples' feet!

An interesting relic of the past, suggestive of the sieges of Jerusalem, is the fragment of an arch, which was, no doubt, the starting-point of the high bridge that rose above a portion of the city, and joined the two great hills on which Jerusalem was built,—Mount Zion and Mount Moriah. It thrills the beholder to stand beside the base of this huge arch, and think that on the bridge it once upheld, the Roman conqueror, Titus, advanced to hold a conference with the leading Jews, when, having

AN INTERESTING RELIC.

captured one-half of Jerusalem, he called upon the other
section to surrender. His offers, however, were treated with
disdain; for trusting still that Israel's God would rescue
them, although the remainder of the city was in ruins, and
though the Romans had already occupied their Holy Temple,
the Jews fought on in desperation, to die by thousands round
the ruined palace of their kings. The world has rarely seen
a more impressive proof of national faith and heroism.

At one place in our walk about the Holy City we saw
some wretched men and women crouching in the sun, and
sheltered by a
mass of paving-
stones. They
called to us in
half-articulate
words, rattled
tin boxes partly
filled with coins,
in appeal for
charity, and
finally held out
for our inspec-

THE LEPER HOSPITAL.

tion fingerless hands and toeless feet. We started back,
regarding them with mingled horror and compassion, for
these we knew must be the hideous lepers of Jerusalem,
about whom we had often read. We threw to them some
pennies, for which they struggled furiously, the helpless and
the disappointed ones uttering meantime heart-rending cries.
Physicians claim that leprosy is not infectious, but we took
care to keep at a safe distance from these loathsome beggars,
and, like the Levite of old, to pass, though sorrowfully, on the
other side. They are, however, genuine objects of compassion, and, as they cannot work, they must be supported
either by the State or by private charity. Accordingly, it was

with satisfaction that we beheld, not far from the Jaffa Gate,
the hospital erected in 1867 for these pitiable creatures.
They should all be secluded there; but liberty is still allowed
them, and they often marry, thus propagating the disease,
since this unfortunate evil is hereditary.

It is not strange to find these lepers in Jerusalem; for,
though by no means limited to the Israelites, that race, when
in the Orient, has always suffered more or less from this ter-

rible malady.
Yet the Mosaic
regulations in
regard to it were
very strict.
Those who had
any symptoms
of it were com-
pelled to show
themselves to
the priest and
undergo a seclu-
sion of seven
days. If they
were then dis-

A STREET IN JERUSALEM.

covered to be really leprous, they were obliged to live outside
the town, crying "Unclean, Unclean," to every one who
might approach them, and dragging out a life of self-abhor-
ring misery, until relieved by a welcome death.

Finally, having made the circuit of Jerusalem, we passed
through one of the gates and found ourselves in a thorough-
fare called David Street. It is precisely in its streets that
the Jerusalem of the present day is disappointing. Outside
the walls, along the line of its historic battlements, or looking on the surrounding hills, which are the same as in the
time of Christ, one feels the dignity and sanctity of the Holy

City, and can understand why it was said to be "Beautiful for situation, the joy of the whole earth," and why the Psalmist cried with passionate enthusiasm: "If I forget thee, O Jerusalem, let my right hand forget her cunning." But in its present ill-paved, narrow streets, swarming with poverty-stricken Hebrews, scowling Turks and half-crazed pilgrims of all nationalities, the traveler is sickened by the filth of the place and

STREET BEGGARS.

wearied by the fraud and fanaticism which everywhere prevail. An effort of the will is needed here to rise above the environing physical and moral degradation, and to derive inspiration from the memory of the scenes which have endeared this city to mankind for nearly twenty centuries. Yet it must be confessed that many of its streets are picturesque. In fact, so narrow are the passageways, and

AS IN A FORTRESS.

so high and gloomy are the adjoining walls, that we continually felt, while walking here, that we were passing through the corridors of some huge fortress. There are few outside windows in the houses, and even these are

VIA DOLOROSA.

either grated or hidden by projecting lattices. Yet one should bear in mind that, in all such Oriental residences, the light and air are gained from inner courtyards. Hence from these unattractive walls and arches one can form no idea of the comfort, and even luxury, which possibly exist within.

The most renowned and sacred street within the Holy City is the Via Dolorosa,—believed by many to be the route along which the Saviour bore His cross to Calvary. If it could be established for a certainty that this was the actual pathway of the Man of Sorrows on His way to death, who could behold it save with tear-dimmed eyes? But it need hardly be remarked that there is no likelihood that such is

ECCE HOMO ARCH.

CHURCH OF MATER DOLOROSA.

HOUSE OF CAIAPHAS.

the case. The general direction of the street may possibly be the same, but its ancient level undoubtedly lies forty or fifty feet below the pavement of to-day. The soil on its surface surmounts the accumulation of the wrecks of centuries.

Nevertheless, at one place the Via Dolorosa is bordered by a structure which has for many generations borne the name of the Ecce Homo Arch, and ⊃ is supposed to mark the spot where Pontius Pilate, pointing to the guiltless prisoner before him, uttered the well-known words,—"Behold the man!" Close by it is a little church, which, like the street itself, is often thronged with pious pilgrims. In fact, almost every foot of the Via Dolorosa is consecrated to some sad event connected with the path to Calvary. Thus, one spot is believed to indicate the place where Jesus took the cross upon His shoulders; another where He fell in weakness; another still where He addressed the women of Jerusalem; and yet another where Veronica, it is said, wiped the perspiration from His brow.

HOUSE OF VERONICA.

In this street also are the houses of Caiaphas and of
Veronica, as well as that of Dives, before which lay the
beggar Lazarus. At a neighboring corner, now lighted by
an ever-burning lamp, Jesus, on His way to Calvary, is said
to have met His Mother. Some twenty feet from this, there
is a slight depression in the wall, to which tradition points
as that caused by Christ's elbow as He pressed against it in
His fall. In sight of this, also, is the stone on which the
thirty pieces of silver were counted out to Judas, as well
as the column on which the cock crew at the denial of Peter.
To some readers the mention of these localities may seem
sacrilegious; but no description of Jerusalem would be complete unless it gave due prominence to these so-called
"Holy Sites," which have been revered for centuries by
thousands. Moreover, though every one of them be discarded as historically valueless, their presence does not impair

THE HOUSE OF DIVES.

the transcendent value of the Christian religion, nor do they in the least detract from the incomparable teachings and in-spiring life of Him who died upon the Cross.

However, concerning one portion of Jerusalem tradition is beyond question trustworthy. It is the area now occupied by the Mosque of Omar. Certain localities in this world have

MOSQUE OF OMAR.

been from earliest times reserved for worship. This hill is one of them. It antedates by many centuries the age of Solomon. Even before the days of Abraham it had been used for sacrificial rites; and to this height that patriarch came and offered up the ram in place of his son Isaac. Years after, in the splendid temple built by Solomon on this site, the solemn ritual of the Jews went on for centuries; and, finally, for more than a thousand years the hill has been a place of worship for the followers of Mohammed.

Eight handsome gateways open into its sacred courtyard. In former times, black dervishes, with drawn daggers, stood

A 'STATION" IN THE VIA DOLOROSA.

day and night beside these gates to keep the sacred precinct unpolluted by the infidel. In fact, till recently, no Christian, with rare exceptions, was permitted to set foot within this hallowed area. But now, save on the occasion of a Moslem festival, the traveler will have no difficulty in entering, if he will pay the required fee. At first it may seem strange that this old Hebrew site should be held sacred by Mohammedans. Yet it is easily understood, when we remember that Mohammed derived most of his religious knowledge from the Jews, and looked upon Jerusalem as a place sanctified by the prayers of Hebrew patriarchs and prophets.

In this connection it is interesting to recall the fact that in their time the Jews were as exclusive as the Moslems. Not long ago an archæologist discovered one of the tablets of the Hebrew Temple, which, verifying the statement of Josephus, forbade strangers to enter the privileged area. It reads as follows: "No foreigner is to step within the balustrade around the temple and

ONE OF THE GATES.

MOSQUE OF OMAR (INTERIOR).

its enclosure. Whoever is caught, will be responsible to himself for his death, which will ensue." This gives a startling reality to the event narrated in the Acts of the Apostles, when Paul, suspected of having introduced a stranger into the Temple, would have been put to death but for the prompt interference of the com- mander of the fortress (the present Tower Antonia), who with his soldiers hastened to Paul's rescue.

TOWER ANTONIA.

The principal building in this great enclosure is the Dome of the Rock, popularly known as the Mosque of Omar. It is a beautiful and graceful structure, embellishing and dignifying the entire city. Unlike most mosques, there rise from it no tapering minarets, with exquisitely chiseled balconies, where the muezzin calls to prayer. Its elegantly modeled dome is deemed sufficient; and this, indeed, though

THE DOME OF THE ROCK.

ninety-six feet in height, is so extremely light and buoyant in appearance, that it would not sur- prise the traveler much to see it rise and float away toward Heaven, as Mo- hammed himself is said to have done from this very spot. The mosque itself is in the form of a richly decorated octagon. The lower half of the walls is covered with white marble, —the upper part is an expanse of porcelain tiles, whose colors blend in harmonious

INTERIOR OF MOSQUE.

though intricate designs. Around them also, like a sculptured frieze of blue and white enameled tiles, are interwoven passages from the Koran.

The theology of the builders of this edifice cannot be misunderstood, for among various verses from the Moslem Scriptures here inscribed, are these:

A MOSLEM SHEIK.

"The Messiah, Jesus, was the son of Mary and Joseph. He was also the ambassador of God. Believe in God and His ambassador, but do not say that God is three. For God is one, and cannot have a son. Pray then to God alone:— That is the only way." Moreover, not content with the religious teachings carved upon the walls, a Moslem priest, from a beautiful marble pulpit in this courtyard, every Friday proclaims to the faithful the significance and sanctity of all around them.

Having exchanged our shoes for slippers, according to the Moslem requirements, lest we should defile this consecrated area, we entered, first, a little gem of architecture, which we supposed to be one of the fountains for ablution always found in the vicinity of mosques. It is, however, an antechamber where the faithful pray before they pass within the mosque itself. This graceful pavilion, the walls of which are all inlaid with exquisite mosaic, bears the name of "David's Judgment Hall," for the Moslems claim that King David formerly hung a chain here as a test of men's veracity. All truthful witnesses could touch it without ill effects; but if a liar handled it, a link fell off at once,—one link for every lie. At this rate it is not surprising that the chain speedily lost its links. They long since disappeared.

THE MARBLE PULPIT.

From this anteroom for prayer, we advanced to and entered the mosque itself. Photography here cannot avail us much. An exceedingly "dim religious light" pervades the sacred edifice. For several minutes we could hardly distin-

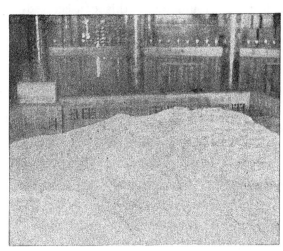

THE ROCK.

guish our surroundings, but presently perceived that we were standing on a marble pavement partly covered with straw matting. We seemed to be in the *foyer* of an amphitheatre. On either side of us was a curving wall, upheld by marble columns. Occasionally a ray of light, through stained glass windows near the roof, revealed some glittering mosaics or a sculptured capital. "Where did these columns come from?" we inquired. "Some of them, doubtless, are relics of the various temples reared here by the Hebrews and their Roman conquerors," was the reply.

We slowly made our way along the serpentine corridor, and gradually understood the singular construction of the edifice. It is built in two concentric circles; the outer wall of the structure being one, and a corresponding circular screen the other; while, in the centre, just beneath the mighty dome, is—what? A precious shrine? By no means. Some noble work of art? Not at all. What then? A bare, rough rock, fifty-six feet in length and forty feet in breadth, without a particle of decoration on its surface.

PLACE OF APPEARANCE TO THE SHEPHERDS.

"What!" we exclaim, "is it to guard a mass of unhewn stone that this magnificent temple has been reared; that these rich columns stand in silent reverence; and that its glittering mosaics and lamps of variously-colored glass recall Aladdin's fabled cave?" Incredible as it seems, such is the fact. For this rock is the natural summit of the hill called Mount Moriah,—a real and tangible relic of the great Jerusalem. It was revered when Abraham and David knelt on it in prayer, when the Ark of the Covenant rested on its summit, and when the Son of Man drove from His Father's house, which then surmounted it, those who had made the place a den of thieves. There seems to be little doubt that when the Jews erected here their wonderful temple, they chose this rock as the foundation of its sacred altar. Beneath it are enormous rock-hewn cisterns, from forty to sixty feet deep, which served as reservoirs of water, or as receptacles for all the sacrificial blood that

UNDER THE ROCK.

flowed in great profusion from the Hebrew Temple. Accordingly, few objects in the world are deemed so sacred as this rock; and few indeed have such good reason to be reverenced. Unfortunately, however, a mass of crude

Mohammedan traditions are connected with it. Thus we had pointed out to us upon its surface the very spots where Abraham, David, Solomon, and Elijah knelt upon the rock to pray. Mohammed also prayed here, and with such earnestness that when he

ascended thence to Heaven, the rock, it is related, started to follow him, and was only held back by the Angel Gabriel, whose fingerprints are now exhibited in the stone.

The Moslems, however, claim that the rock, uplifted thus, never returned to its original position, and is even now suspended in the air! There is, in fact, beneath it a small cave, known as the Sepulchre of Solomon. Into the

ENTRANCE TO CHURCH OF THE HOLY SEPULCHRE.

rock above this, Mohammed is said to have driven some nails, which gradually work through the stone and drop into the tomb below. When all the nails shall have disappeared, the Prophet will return to announce the end of the world. Three nails are still intact, but we were told that a fourth is on its way downward. The Moslem attenuant, therefore, warns all pilgrims to step lightly, lest they shake a nail through, and thus hasten the day of judgment.

As the Dome of the Rock is the building which Moslems deem most sacred in Jerusalem, so the one most reverenced by Christians is the Church of the Holy Sepulchre, erected by the Emperor Constantine, about three hundred years after the Crucifixion. It has no architectural beauty. Beyond an open space, where petty traders vend their rosaries and trinkets with discordant voices in almost every language known to man, is a façade which does not in the least suggest the entrance to a religious shrine. There were originally two portals here, but one has been walled up, thus making the building unsymmetrical. Three marble columns flank the open door on either side. One of them has a crack in it; and it is believed that from this rift, on the Judgment Day, will leap forth the fire that is to destroy the world. Accordingly, the riven shaft has been for centuries kissed by pious pilgrims, till now its surface is as smooth as glass. It is well to observe this at the outset, for every traveler should prepare himself for what he is to encounter in the Church of the

ROOF OF THE CHURCH OF THE HOLY SEPULCHRE.

Holy Sepulchre, before he sets foot beyond its threshold.   If
he is satisfied that what he is to see is genuine, then let him
enter the church filled with enthusiasm, reverence and joy.
If, on the contrary, he feels that much of it is the result of

A GUARD.

ignorance and fraud, he should
not lose his temper, but should
pass in, philosophically and
quietly, as to a study of
humanity, remembering, above
all, that the hallowing influence of those events in Christ's
life which occurred somewhere
upon this rocky platform of
Jerusalem, should not be less-
ened because of the superstition of a portion of His followers.

The Church of the Holy
Sepulchre is not so much a
church, as a sacred exposition
building.   Its enormous roof
covers a multitude of altars, chapels, stairways, caves and
natural elevations; and under this one canopy, as if miracu-
lously concentrated into a small area, are gathered almost all
the places mentioned in the Bible, which could by any pos-
sibility be located in Jerusalem. The "Holy Sites" are
owned by various Christian sects, who hate each other cor-
dially; so much so, indeed, that officers, appointed by the
Turkish Government, are always present to protect the
property, and to prevent the owners from flying at one
another's throats. This is, alas! no exaggeration, for deeds of
bloodshed and violence have frequently occurred here, especially during the Easter celebrations.   Not long ago, during
Holy Week, a priest of the Greek Church hurled a bottle of

ink at the head of the Franciscan Superior who was conducting a procession round the Holy Sepulchre. It missed the
leader and struck only a deacon; but, though the mark at-
tained was a less shining one, it created a disturbance which
Turkish soldiers were obliged to quell.

After crossing the threshold of this edifice, and passing by
the Moslem guards who are always stationed here to preserve order, the first object we beheld was an altar built
against the wall. Above it hung an almost indistinguishable
painting. Before it was a line of gilded lamps, and under
these a smooth, white stone. "What is this?" we inquired
in a whisper of our guide. "It is the Stone of Unction," he
replied, "on which the body of Jesus was placed by Nicodemus to be anointed for burial." While we were looking

at this slab, a
Russian pilgrim
crept up on his
knees and care-
fully measured
it with a string,
amid repeated
kisses.

"Why does
he do that?"
we queried.

"He is meas-
uring it," was
the reply, "in
order to have
his winding-

THE STONE OF UNCTION.

sheet made of precisely the same dimensions." A few steps
from this is the spot where the Mother of Jesus stood while
the body of Christ was being anointed. Close by this
was another shrine, known as the "Chapel of the Parted

Raiment." It is supposed to mark the precise spot where
the garments of Jesus were by lot distributed among the
Roman soldiers. It is the property of the Armenians,
and has been recognized as sacred for six hundred years.
Near this are other chapels, denoting, respectively, the
places where Christ was crowned with thorns, where He

CHAPEL OF SCOURGING.

was scourged, where He was nailed to the Cross, where He
appeared to Mary Magdalene after His Resurrection, and
where the Roman Centurion stood, during the Crucifixion;
and, finally, we were shown a stone in which are two impres-
sions, said to have been made by the Saviour's wounded feet.
We next descended a stairway, thirty feet in length, which
led to the Chapel of St. Helena. This is the property of the
Abyssinian Christians, and is revered by all the Christian
sects; for here, it is said, Helena, the mother of Constantine,
sat while directing the excavations which resulted in the
finding of the Cross of Christ.

From this chapel we descended fifteen feet further, to reach what is said to be the identical place where, after persistent digging, the true Cross was brought to light, though it had been buried for three hundred years. The Empress Helena plays an important part in the history of Christianity. She was not merely the mother of the first Christian Emperor; she must also be called the mother of most of the church traditions which have had their origin in Palestine. Thus, in this particular spot, it is stated that she found all three of the crosses—those upon which hung the two thieves, as well as that of Christ. The problem was to know which

A GREEK PRIEST.

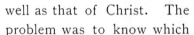

was the sacred one. To settle this, they were all taken to the bedside of a devout woman who was very ill. When she beheld the first cross she became a raving maniac. They therefore tried the second one. Immediately she went into fearful spasms, and six strong men could hardly hold her. Naturally they were afraid to bring in the third cross. Still, as she seemed about to die, they agreed that the third could do no more than put her out of misery. Accordingly, they brought it in, and at once the afflicted woman was completely restored. The cross which cured her, therefore, was proclaimed to be the Cross of Christ.

A SYRIAN BISHOP.

In another part of the church is the Chapel of the Crucifixion, where one beholds what is alleged to be the very Rock of Calvary. In this is shown (at present bordered by a rim of gold) the rent made in its surface by the earthquake that

THE HOLY SEPULCHRE.

occurred at the time of the Crucifixion. Nay, more than this, one can look down into the very hole in which the Cross is said to have been placed!

Not far from here we saw the chapel said to contain the grave of our first parent, Adam. Every reader will recall the tear which Mark Twain here dropped in memory of our common ancestor; and to a

rational mind nothing could seem more absurd than locating the grave of Adam near the site of Calvary. But we must bear in mind that, to a large proportion of mankind, only "seeing is believing." For fifteen hundred years the majority of pilgrims to the Holy Land, coming from the steppes of Russia, from the mountains of Syria, from Egypt, and even from Abyssinia, expected and demanded to see all the localities mentioned in the Bible. This demand inevitably created the supply, in order to satisfy those who probably needed some such tangible souvenirs to help them to appreciate and understand the life of Him whom they were taught to reverence. Inspired by intense religious zeal, the early pilgrims and Crusaders must have gone about Jerusalem intoxicated with their own enthusiasm, and utterly undirected by a critical spirit of investigation. Hence, as years rolled by, the influence of tradition and antiquity gave to these places a sanctity which it is now almost impossible to disturb.

The tomb of Adam is the property of the Greeks, who are so proud of it that it is somewhat surprising that their discomfited rivals have not produced the grave of Mother Eve! As an instance of the sectarian jealousy that prevails here, it may be stated that the Greek Christians, in 1808, actually destroyed the authentic monuments of the Crusaders, Godfrey de Bouillon and King Baldwin I, for the sole reason that, if left here, the Latin Church, through some technicality, would claim the site. There is little doubt, moreover, that one of the causes of the Crimean War was the contentions of the Christian sects in Palestine — Russia supporting the Greek Church, and France defending the Latins.

INTERIOR OF THE HOLY SEPULCHRE.

But of all places in this famous building, the most revered is the Holy Sepulchre. It is a little chapel, built of highly-colored limestone, twenty-six feet in length by eighteen feet in breadth. Though it has frequently fallen into ruin and been rebuilt (the present structure dates only from the year 1808), the site which it still covers has not changed for fifteen hundred years. One gazes on it, therefore, with the deepest interest, for (genuine or not) no spot on earth has so profoundly influenced the fate of Christian nations. It brought about one of the most important events of the Middle Ages — the Crusades; and for its possession and defense the best and bravest blood in Christendom was freely shed. Other than Christian blood has also flowed in its vicinity. For on the 15th of July, 1099, the victorious Crusaders, having finally captured Jerusalem, put to death most of the Turkish population, and then approached the Holy Sepulchre barefooted and singing hymns of praise. As we drew near it, a line of pilgrims stood in front of us; another line formed quickly in our rear—all eagerly awaiting

GREEK PRIESTS.

the moment when their turn would come to pass within. Several men, as well as women, were weeping and moaning at this realization of a life-long dream. At last my turn came, and with a feeling of awe, never experienced before or since, I stepped alone across the threshold. I found myself at first in a little vestibule, ablaze with gilded lamps. Before me was a piece of rock encased in marble. It is said to be the stone which the angel rolled away from the mouth of the sepulchre. Advancing still farther, I stood within a tiny, marble-lined compartment, only seven feet long and six feet wide. The air was heavy and oppressive, for hanging from the ceiling, which I could easily touch with my hand, were forty-three golden lamps, kept constantly burning. Of

SERVICE AT THE HOLY SEPULCHRE.

these, thirteen belong to the Latins, thirteen to the Greeks, thirteen to the Armenians, and four to the Copts. This inner room is supposed to be the veritable rock-hewn tomb of Jesus, and on a platform, two feet high and six feet long, is a marble slab, which covers the rock on which the Saviour's lifeless body is said to have reposed. It has been worn as smooth as glass by the kisses of millions. I was allowed to remain here but a moment, since others were impatient for my place. Accordingly, returning to the body of the church, I looked attentively at those who stood in line, seeking admission to the Sepulchre. Of course, among so many nationalities there is great diversity, but there were many pilgrims whom I would rather not meet alone on a dark night. There is a saying in the Orient that the worst Moslems are the ones who have been in Mecca, and the worst Christians those who have seen Jerusalem. Still another proverb says: "If thy neighbor has made one pilgrimage, distrust him; if he has made two, make haste to sell thy house." We can the more readily believe this when we

STREET NEAR THE HOLY SEPULCHRE.

recall the scenes which take place around the Holy Sepulchre at every Easter festival. For then the miracle of the "Holy Fire," as it is called may well make angels weep and all intelligent Christians shudder with disgust. The Roman

Catholic and Armenian Christians discarded this function three hundred years ago, denouncing it as a gross imposture; but the Greek Church still maintains it.

During the entire day and night before Easter the immense Church of the Holy Sepulchre is literally packed with pilgrims. They stand there for hours without food or drink, and gradually work themselves into a frenzy by shrieks and howls, and a monotonous wail of *"Hada-Ku-ba-Said-Na"*—"This is the Tomb of the Lord." Some of these enthusiasts have come thousands of miles to obtain the "sacred fire," and are determined to do so if it costs them their lives. Such persons, if they have not a good position, climb up on the

RIOTING AT THE SEPULCHRE.

shoulders of their weaker neighbors, and run on toward the Sepulchre on the heads of others, descending finally into the already compact mass in the midst of frightful confusion and violence.

At length, about two o'clock in the afternoon, the Greek Patriarch goes within the Sepulchre. There is now a period of breathless silence, almost appalling after all the pandemonium that has prevailed. Presently, nobody knows exactly why, it is rumored that the Holy Ghost has descended to the Sepulchre in a tongue of flame. A moment more, and four or five lighted torches are thrust out through the holes which perforate the chapel-walls. Language fails to depict the scene that follows. Ten thousand men immediately contend like maniacs to get their tapers lighted. Twenty thousand arms leap forward toward the torches of the priests, like the leafless branches of a forest swayed by a tornado. Hysterical fanatics rush about, searing themselves with lighted tapers, as a kind of penance. Many are trampled under foot, and some are even crushed to death. On one occasion, three hundred pilgrims perished in the church. In 1895, until suppressed by the soldiers of the Sultan, two rival Christian factions fought here desperately.

It is a painful thought that Turkish guards must be stationed here to check the rioting and fighting of Christians. For, in their act of guardianship, they smile sarcastically at the so-called followers of the Prince of Peace. If He should once more appear upon Mount Zion, He would no doubt rebuke these poor misguided worshipers, by whom, perhaps, He would be murdered again, upon the site of His reputed grave! "Such" says Dean Stanley, "is the Greek Easter, the greatest moral argument against the identity of

TOMB OF DAVID.

the spot which it professes to honor. Considering the place, the time, and the intention of the professed miracle, it is probably the most offensive imposture to be found in the world.''

A JEWISH WOMAN.

The question which, above all others, suggests itself to the visitor to the Holy Sepulchre is, ''Can we believe that this is the real burial-place of Jesus?'' Sad as it is to think of such continued and wide-spread delusion, there is not, in the writer's opinion, any satisfactory proof that Christ was either crucified or buried within the precincts, or indeed in the immediate neighbor-hood, of this church. There is no need to enumerate here the vexed arguments for and against the belief; but one thing can be made quite clear in half-a-dozen sentences. The Gospels state that Christ was crucified and buried outside the city walls. But look from any eminence in Jerusalem and see how far in toward the centre of the city stands the church of the Holy Sepulchre. Can we suppose that the boundary lines of this illustrious capital in the period of its glory were narrower than they are to-day,—especially when the valleys which surround Jerusalem leave it but one direction for expansive growth? Besides this, the historical evidence in favor of the Holy Sepulchre is also unsatisfactory. It is remarkable that no description of the locality of the tomb of Jesus is given either by the Gospel writers, or by St. Paul, who visited Jerusalem at least twice after his conversion. Why was this? Undoubtedly because to them the death and burial of Christ were insignificant facts

POOL OF BETHESDA.

compared with His resurrection.   The early Christians all believed that Jesus was to return before their generation passed
away.   They therefore gave no thought to the poor
place wherein their Master's body had reposed for three
days.   They could have no conception of the centuries
to come, in which man's reverence for sacred sites would
lead him to seek out this sepulchre.   Enough for them
that Christ had risen from the grave and was to reappear at

any moment in
the clouds of
Heaven.

Yet, while re-
flecting on the
m i l l i o n s who
have come to
Palestine to see
what they be-
lieved to be the
actual sepulchre
of the Son of

GOLGOTHA.

God, we are forced to ask ourselves — Can it be possible
that a delusion has exerted such a mighty influence in
human history?   But it was not the actual sepulchre
(genuine or false) which revolutionized the minds of men,
it was the idea behind it.   The fact that Moslems held this land
to the exclusion of Christ's followers, is what aroused the
Christian world to take up arms, and led to Palestine the
legions of the Cross.   The one essential thing was the idea;
for, as Napoleon truly said, "Imagination rules the world."

In the opinion of many students and travelers—including
the writer of these pages,—the probable site of Calvary is a
remarkably formed cliff, a little beyond the Damascus Gate,
which from a distance bears a striking resemblance to a
death's-head, with natural caverns in the rock suggestive of

eyeless sockets. Since the outlines of this hillock are to-day almost certainly what they were nineteen hundred years ago, it would not be strange if it had then been popularly called Golgotha, "the place of a skull." There evidently *was* a place

THE MOUNT OF OLIVES.

so called, out-side the city of Jerusalem, and the peculiar con-formation of this knoll would justify the name to-day. It must always have been outside the walls, yet, from its nearness to the Damascus Gate, it would have been con-tiguous to one of the great thoroughfares to Jerusalem, so that "the passers by" could easily have "railed on him." Moreover, this skull-shaped cliff was then, as it is now, in a very con-spicuous position; and the Saviour's form upon the Cross would have been plainly visible to the "people who stood beholding," and to the "women looking on afar off."

Of all the hills that rise around Jerusalem beyond the deep ravines, which form almost a circle about the city, the most profoundly interesting is, of course, the Mount of Olives. Passing from the uncertainties of the Holy Sepul-chre, one looks on this with genuine satisfaction, for of its authenticity there can be no doubt. The eighteen centuries which have come and gone since Jesus was wont to retire to its slopes at eventide for prayer and contemplation, can have made little difference in its form. It is true, the palm-trees that once flourished here, from which the exultant multitude plucked branches to adorn the path of Christ on His triumphal entry into Jerusalem, have disappeared, and there are now few olive groves to justify its name; but it is nevertheless *the very hill* associated with so many thrilling scenes in the life of Christ. Probably, too, the general direction of the road that crosses it is the same as when the Saviour trod it on His way to Bethany. Moreover, at the foot of Olivet is a little area, enclosed in whitewashed walls. This is the reputed Garden of Gethsemane. The traveler may enter it, for courteous Franciscan monks are always in attendance. My first impression here was one of disappointment. The modern-looking pathways lined with flowers, the plants, and carefully trimmed hedges,—what had these to do with the historic Garden of Gethsemane? The conservatory in the corner, also, where the monks cultivate their choicest flowers, seemed painfully unsuited to a place whose principal characteristics were undoubtedly retirement and purely natural surroundings. But the monks maintain that to cultivate flowers here is certainly no

GETHSEMANE.

sin, especially as every visitor buys some; while the fine olive-oil yielded by the trees, and the numerous rosaries manufactured from the olive-stones, are also sold at a high price. One must live, they argue, even upon the slopes of Olivet.

Within this enclosure there are a number of old olive-trees, which are said to be the very ones within whose shadow Jesus knelt in spiritual anguish. But this is quite impossible. It is well known that both Titus and

THE GARDEN.

Hadrian, in their successive conquests of Jerusalem, cut down all the trees in its vicinity, and the Crusaders found this region well-nigh destitute of wood. Still, since it is characteristic of the olive to sprout repeatedly from the same roots, even though cut off at the ground, it is not wholly improbable that these trees have sprung from the ones beneath which on the midnight air were uttered the agonizing words: ''Father, if it be possible, let this cup pass from me!''

But can we believe that this is the exact locality of Gethsemane? We know, at least, that somewhere in this valley at the base of Olivet, and just

POOL OF SILOAM.

MOUNT OF OLIVES FROM JERUSALEM.

across the brook Kedron, was the secluded spot whither the
Master came with His disciples after the Last Supper.   But
whether this is the *precise* location is uncertain.   The Greeks,
for example, have their Garden of Gethsemane a little farther
up the hill, and are, of course, confident that theirs is the
right one.   To thoughtful and intelligent travelers it should
be enough that somewhere in this limited area (the whole
of which is, in a moment, open to the gaze) occurred that
scene, whose narrative for over eighteen centuries has moved
unnumbered listeners and readers to repentant tears.

When one seats himself in a retired portion of the Mount
of Olives and looks out on the historic landscape, he realizes
that it is the natural features and associations of the Holy
Land that really give him pleasure.   The life which consecrated these Judæan Hills may not have left a trace within
the church of the Holy Sepulchre, but it has made each portion of the Mount of Olives consecrated ground.   No part of
Palestine is hallowed by so many memories of Jesus as this
hill; for to its olive groves He often came to escape the noise
and turmoil of the city, and here He uttered words familiar
now to millions of our race.   It was from Olivet that He
gazed tenderly   upon Jerusalem
and   wept

PLACE OF THE TREASON OF JUDAS.

as He foretold its doom.   Here also, more than anywhere
else on earth, He held communion with His Father, thus
gaining strength and inspiration for His life and death; and
we are told that on some portion of this hill, having conducted His disciples out toward Bethany, He gave to them
His benediction and parted from them forever.

CHURCH OF THE ASCENSION.

Unfortunately, however, though there is surely enough
material here for true religious sentiment, it by no means
satisfies the average pilgrim.   Upon the crest of Olivet,
therefore, has been built the "Church of the Ascension."
On entering this, we saw in the floor a small, rectangular
space, surrounded by a marble coping.   Pilgrims were pros-
trating themselves before it and kissing the pavement repeatedly.   The cause was soon explained to us, for in the pavement is shown a slight irregularity, believed to be the imprint
made by the right foot of Jesus as He left the earth.

This is an admirable illustration of Palestine, as *men* have made it. Practically disregarding the hill itself, which is unquestionably genuine, thousands of pilgrims prefer to crawl beneath an arch of masonry to worship so-called footprints in a stone! There are three kinds of travelers in the Holy Land. First,

THE FOOTPRINT.

those who are wisely content to see the natural localities connected with the life of Christ, and therefore gain from Palestine the solemn inspiration of its priceless memories; secondly, those who lose themselves within the slough of superstition there; and thirdly, those who, thoroughly offended by the false, forget the value of the true, and ridicule it all.

BETHANY.

Just beyond the crest of Olivet lies the little village of
Bethany. Its site is undoubtedly authentic, and we are
sure, beyond peradventure, that it was over this same hill,
and to this very place, that Jesus loved to come to find rest
in the home of his friends, Lazarus, Martha and Mary. The
most satisfactory thing, however, for the traveler to do here,
is to survey from a distance the town and the surrounding
hills, whose contours have remained unchanged, and then to
retire. For, if he persists in going nearer, he will experience

HOUSE OF LAZARUS.

the usual dis-
enchantment.
The modern
Bethany is
a cluster of
miserable huts,
without a build-
ing which seems
to be more than
a century old.
Nevertheless, a
swarm of blear-
eyed, ragged children greeted us here with cries of "Backsheesh, Backsheesh! Tombo Lazarus! Tombo Lazarus!"
For not only are the ruins of the house of Martha and Mary
pointed out, but also the tomb from which Lazarus is said
to have come forth at the divine command.

We were foolish enough to visit the so-called tomb; and
descending by candle-light twenty-five slippery steps, we
reached what seemed to have been originally the bottom of a
well.

Again, therefore, at Bethany, as in so many other places
in the Holy Land, we see that "the letter killeth, the spirit
giveth life." In a broad sense, Palestine is still the land of
Jesus. In a narrow sense, it is not so at all. It is a pic-

TOMB OF THE VIRGIN.

ture of which only the grand outlines are satisfactory. It is sublime in its entirety, but tawdry in detail. Even supposing that the precise localities connected with the life and death of Christ are still capable of identification after the dreadful sieges and disasters that have come upon them, the question arises, Which guide or scholar should we follow of all who have written on Jerusalem? There are hardly two of them who do not fight each other fiercely, like ecclesiastical gladiators in an arena of uncertainty. The part of wisdom, therefore, in such a country, where almost every stone is made to indicate some sacred spot, which every other sect immediately disputes, is to fix one's gaze upon the unchanging natural features and draw from them the interest their unrivaled history inspires.

The religion of Jesus, which still lives in the hearts of millions, is not dependent on the existence of old sepulchres and shrines. Its essential monuments are not tombs, but characters; not perishable temples upon earth, but a city of God, "not made with hands, eternal in the heavens." Returning from Bethany and Olivet, and walking down the valley of the Kedron, beyond the reputed Tomb of the Virgin, we came upon a singular monument,— the greater part of which is a mass of solid rock, about twenty feet square, completely detached from the adjoining cliff. Within

AT THE BASE OF OLIVET.

it is a compartment, eight feet square, with spaces on the sides for two sarcophagi. Originally, it must have been im-posing, for it is fifty feet in height, and was adorned with columns and a delicately sculptured frieze. As we were passing it, our guide picked up a stone and hurled it at the monument, spitting meantime upon the ground and uttering a curse. "What are you doing?" we inquired: "what is the meaning of that heap of stones to which you have just added one?" He turned and spat again. "It is the tomb of Ab-salom," he said. In fact, both Jews and Moslems believe that this surmounts the grave of David's disobedient son, and they take a singular delight in showing thus their detestation of treachery to a father.

Not far from this, we paused to notice on the side of Olivet two other monuments. One, like the tomb of Absalom, is an enormous block of stone hewn out of the adjoining cliff; the other is distinguished by a colonnade, behind which, in the hillside, is a kind of catacomb. Nothing is known with certainty about these sepulchres. The names assigned to them are based on no authority save that of vague tradition. But they, of course, must have some legendary history to satisfy the memento - craving pilgrim. Hence

TOMBS OF THE KINGS.

one is called the "Tomb of Zachariah;" the other, the "Grotto of St. James," from the belief that the Apostle James concealed himself there after the Crucifixion.

We lingered here some time absorbed in thought; for although nothing is known of those who were originally buried here, one interesting fact gives to these tombs along the slope of Olivet a priceless value. It is that they were undoubtedly standing here at the time of Christ. Ruin, we know, soon overtook alike the glorious Temple and the buildings of the city, of which, as Holy Writ affirms, not one stone was to be left upon another; but these old rock-hewn sepulchres remain almost unchanged since Jesus walked beside them. Upon these very structures, therefore, He must have looked; and this fact gives to them a value shared,

ENTRANCE TO QUARRY.

with certainty, by nothing else of human workmanship in the world. Around them, for some distance, the hill is almost concealed under prostrate tombstones. They mark the burial-place of Jews who have by thousands toiled back to Jerusalem, content if finally their dust might mingle with the soil of their native land.

In our walks around Jerusalem we often found ourselves before huge openings in the hillsides. One of these is called the "Tombs of the Kings." Whether or not authentic names have been attached to them, certain it is that all the hills around Jerusalem are honey-combed with rock-hewn sepulchres of great antiquity. They are of every shape and size. Some have fine carvings chiseled in

THE GROTTO OF JEREMIAH.

the stone. The cost of making many of them proves that persons of great wealth or rank were buried here. Some of their entrances seem to have been closed by stone doors turning on socket-hinges, and fastened by bolts on the inside. Strangely enough, no inscriptions tell the names of their former inmates or even the dates of their entomb-

POOL OF HEZEKIAH.

ment, and now the sepulchres are tenantless alike of earthly treasure and of human dust.

But sepulchres are not the only excavations in these hills. Among them are the royal quarries, where architects obtained the enormous blocks of limestone for the walls and Temple of Jerusalem. The evidence is abundant that skilful stone-cutters once labored in these rock-hewn labyrinths, and that in many instances the blocks were carried forth, all carved and ready for their appointed place. This, therefore,

verifies the statement of the Scriptures that, in the building
of the Temple, the stones were all prepared before being
brought there; so that neither hammer, nor ax, nor any
tool of iron was heard within the sacred precincts during its

ONE OF THE POOLS OF SOLOMON.

construction. One of these quarries is known as the "Grotto
of Jeremiah," and in its gloomy shadows the prophet is said
to have written his Book of Lamentations.

Jerusalem has never had a natural supply of water sufficient for its needs. King Hezekiah did much to improve the
city in this respect, and Solomon built reservoirs in the hills
ten miles away,—still known as the Pools of Solomon,—from
which ingeniously constructed aqueducts brought a copious
flow of water both to Bethlehem and Jerusalem. For centuries, however, these well-built conduits have been in ruins.
Now and then one or another of them has been repaired and
rendered serviceable, but negligence has soon allowed it to
relapse into its former useless state. The so-called "Pool of
Hezekiah" in Jerusalem is an open tank, capable of contain-

ing four million gallons of water; but this too is in bad repair, the bottom is covered with vegetable mold, and since it is surrounded by houses, the water it contains is often foul. Few people use it, save for washing purposes; but, in summer, when there is a scarcity of water in Jerusalem, the poorer classes sometimes drink it with evil consequences.

The Pool of Bethesda is in a still worse condition, since it has no water at all, is largely filled with rubbish, and even

POOL OF GIHON.

receives the drainage from the neighboring dwellings. It is a melancholy illustration of decadence that the city of Solomon, which was three thousand years ago abundantly supplied with water, and boasted of its pools of Gihon, Solomon and Siloam, is now chiefly dependent upon private wells and cisterns.

No visit to Jerusalem would be complete that did not include an inspection of some of the places of transcendent interest, lying within a radius of a few miles of the Holy City,—Jericho, the Jordan, the Dead Sea, Mar Saba, Bethlehem, and Hebron. Excursions to these localities may be easily made on horseback, even by ladies unaccustomed to that form of exercise; and, on a journey thither, the nights spent in water-proof tents, carpeted with rugs and furnished with every needed comfort, are among the pleasantest memories of a tour in Palestine.   The distance from Jerusalem to

A BEDOUIN.

Jericho, as the crow flies, is only thirteen miles. Few routes, however, are more precipitous and rough; for the Plain of Jericho is thirty-six hundred and twenty feet lower than Mount Zion. Moreover, the road is still so dangerous that one is even more likely now, than in the time of the Good Samaritan, to fall among thieves in making the journey. The traveler's safety, therefore, lies in being openly robbed at the start, by purchasing protection from the Bedouins who practically levy blackmail on all tourists.   There is, however, honor among thieves; and the Arab tribes that inhabit the hill-country of Judæa agree not to molest the traveler, if one of their chiefs has been retained by a sufficient fee.

When I first looked upon the distant Plain of Jericho from the mountains east of Jerusalem, it appeared remarkably beautiful, and I could understand why it had once been called the "Garden of the World," and Jericho itself the "City of Palms."   In fact, palms are known to have been in

THE DEAD SEA.

existence here as late as the time of the Crusaders, who also found under them some lovely flowers, which they called "Jericho roses."

But, with the exception of the site of Ephesus, in Asia Minor, it would be difficult to find a more impressive contrast between past magnificence and present squalor than at Jericho. Its history has been eventful. It was the first city conquered by the Jews when they entered Palestine, fifteen hundred years before the birth of Christ; and from that time, for nearly twenty centuries, it was noted for its wealth and luxury. Under the Roman conquerors of Syria it was rebuilt, and Antony, who for the sake of Cleopatra had "madly flung a world away," gave Jericho to that enchantress of the Nile, as her special property, as one might offer to one's love a costly gem. Its palm-girt and well-irrigated plain was made world-famous by its palaces, gardens and amphitheatres, and here the Roman governor, Herod, died. When Christ passed through it on His last journey to Jerusalem, it was at the height of its splendor and prosperity,—but to-day, of all its opulence not a trace remains.

Some wretched huts clinging, like barnacles, to the Moslem tower called the House of Zacchæus, are all that now remain to hint

JERICHO.

to us that this was once inhabited by man, and the occupants of these hovels are the most repulsive and degraded inhabitants of Syria.

Not far from Jericho, a short ride brings the traveler to the River Jordan. It is by no means an imposing stream,

being here only about thirty or forty feet wide, and as muddy
as the Tiber.   The current is impetuous, and dangerous for
bathers, unless they are expert swimmers.   A considerable
number of pilgrims are drowned in it every year, and we saw
one dead body caught in the bushes on the opposite shore.

Thousands of
Christian pil-
grims come an-
nually, especial-
ly at Easter
time, to bathe
in the sacred
stream ; each
sect having a
different bath-
ing-place, which
each affirms to
be the exact
spot where Jesus
was baptized by

A MIDDAY MEAL IN PALESTINE.

John the Baptist.   On the occasions of these pilgrimages,
the Turkish Government guarantees, as it has done for
centuries, the protection of the Christians from the Bedouins.
To most of the pilgrims to the Holy Land baptism, or even
a bath, in the Jordan is one of the most sacred and important events of their lives, and they religiously cherish the
robes in which they have been immersed, to serve ulti-
mately as their winding-sheets.   Most of them also take
back to their homes bottles filled with water from the sacred
river.   The Jordan has been sometimes praised as being
beautiful and limpid, and such perhaps it may be in the
earlier portion of its course, but we agreed that we had never
seen a stream more desolate and dreary.   One might imagine
that it has a presentiment here of the awful fate which

awaits it close at hand, of being stifled in the brine of the
Dead Sea. Swift and sullen, it here rolls through a land
of desolation to a sea of death.

The first glimpse of the Dead Sea, as we descended
toward it from the site of Jericho, was a great surprise. It
seemed to us as fair a sheet of bright green water as we had
ever looked upon, and it sparkled in the sunlight like a limpid
lake. Could it be possible, we asked ourselves in astonish-
ment, that this was the Dead Sea? When we arrived at its
shore, however, there was no longer any doubt. It was the
climax of the dreary plain over which we had come. There

THE JORDAN.

was no sail upon its surface, no sign of life within its waves.
Some shrub-like vegetation fringed the shore, but that, like
everything else in the vicinity, was covered with a white,
salt crust, and looked as if it had been smitten with leprosy,
while branches of dead trees, brought hither by the Jordan,

lay on the sterile shore like the distorted limbs of monsters
that had died in agony.

The Dead Sea fills the deepest depression known on the
surface of the earth, and is sunk, like a monstrous cauldron,
between mountains three and four thousand feet in height.

GUIDES.

It is nearly four
thousand feet
below the city
of Jerusalem,
which is only
twenty miles
away, and thir-
teen hundred
feet below the
level of the
Mediterranean.
We found
its atmosphere
even in mid-
winter extremely sultry; and in summer, after long months
of exposure to the full power of the sun, it must be almost
unendurable. Of course, we tried a bath in its waters. It
was a singular experience. To go beyond one's depth one
must wade out to a great distance. In doing so, however,
there is no danger, as it is impossible for a person to
sink, so saline is the water. We found it even hard to
swim, owing to the difficulty of keeping our feet under water.
At every stroke we found that we were merely kicking the
air. It might be possible to dive, but we preferred that some
one else should make the experiment, for the salty ingre-
dients are disagreeable enough upon the skin, without allow-
ing them to enter one's eyes, nose and mouth. On coming
out from the bath, our sensations can best be described by
saying that we felt as if we had been immersed in mucilage.

The Dead Sea is the Greek, and comparatively modern, epithet applied to this vast lake. The Hebrews called it the Salt Sea. As is well-known, it has no outlet, and all the water which it receives from the Jordan and other streams is carried off by evaporation. This alone might not explain its extraordinary saltness, which is nearly seven times greater than that of the ocean; but to this there is added another reason, in the fact that at one end of it is a salt deposit, several miles long. Great as is the depression of the surface, its own depth is also enormous, being in one place no less than thirteen hundred feet.

From the Dead Sea our route led upward through the wilderness of Judæa. Neither words nor views can adequately represent the desolation of this frightful area, seamed

with a thousand sterile gorges. Even the Sahara is less dreary. The African desert has a certain beauty in its boundless sweep of sand, now level as the surface of a tranquil sea, now rising into gently rolling waves. But the Judæan

THE WILDERNESS OF JUDÆA.

wilderness is a series of absolutely barren and appalling mountains, divided from each other by great chasms, flanked with frowning precipices, as if the country had been gashed and scarred by demons. It would be like a horrible nightmare to think of being lost in these Judæan cañons,

THE CELL OF SAINT SABA.

where every drop of water is drained away, every vestige of vegetation has vanished, and nothing is visible but yellow, burning sand and rocks. Birds, beasts and men shun the region, as if smitten of God. It was in this wilderness that Jesus is supposed to have fasted forty days; and it is difficult to imagine any one, human or divine, doing anything else in such a place. From the earliest centuries of Christianity ascetics and anchorites have resorted to this wilderness for fasting and prayer, and one old monastery still remains, clinging, as it has done for ages, to the barren rocks. It is the monastery of Mar Saba. From the precipitous cliff, on which it hangs like a wasp's nest, one can

MONASTERY OF MAR

APPROACH TO BETHLEHEM.

drop a stone more than a thousand feet into the sombre
depths of a chasm. Here, in the fourth century after Christ,
the monk, Saint Saba, came to live in solitude and spend
his days in prayer. Eventually hundreds followed him, and
made for themselves homes in the recesses of this frightful
gorge. At last, for mutual preservation from starvation

BETHLEHEM.

and protection from the Bedouins, this
monastery rose, strong as a fortress,
and almost as substantial as the cliffs themselves. Sentinels
are always on duty at its iron gate, through which alone an
entrance can be gained. We were admitted only when our
dragoman had satisfied those within as to who we were.
Never can I forget the night spent at Mar Saba. The rock-
hewn rooms in which we lodged, the bell that called the
monks to midnight prayer and rang out weirdly on the
desert air, and the pity inspired by the lonely ascetic life of
these poor monks,— made the few hours passed in this
Judæan monastery among the most impressive of my life.

Leaving Mar Saba early the next morning, we gradually rode up from the wilderness, and far on in the day beheld, framed in a mass of old gray olive trees illumined by the setting sun, a village which we knew was Bethlehem. Surely if any place on earth should breathe of peace and good-will to mankind, it is this town of David, consecrated by the birth of Christ. But, alas! the reception given us was anything but peaceful. A veritable mob of beggars and street venders swarmed out to meet us on the road, and, in an uproarious babel of strange tongues they thrust upon us rosaries, crosses, beads, stars, canes and numberless other trinkets, all of which they declared were sacred, since they had rested on the Star of the Nativity. Our dragoman did not hesitate to strike a number of these hawkers with his whip, and I remember seeing one of them receive a cut across the face which must have disfigured him for many a day.

It is said that the inhabitants of Bethlehem are the fiercest and most lawless of any in Judæa, and that in riots and other disturbances they are invariably the ringleaders. Our own experience was sufficiently depressing, and, even now, it is impossible for any of our party to recall Bethlehem without the remem-   brance of
that   noisy

CHURCH OF THE NATIVITY.

and persistent mob, whose vociferations were still ringing in
our ears as we finally hastened through the door, and entered
the Church of the Nativity. It is an enormous edifice,
consisting of a church and three convents, belonging respectively to the Latins, the Greeks, and the Armenians. Here,
as in the Church of the Holy Sepulchre at Jerusalem, every

spot that can be
thought of in
connection with
the birth of
Jesus is pointed
out. Thus we
were shown the
place where the
three wise men
knelt, to give
their presents to
the new-born
child. This is
marked by a
marble slab, and

CHAPEL OF THE NATIVITY.

is surmounted by a painting representing the scene. Near
this is the spot where the horses of the Magi were fed; the
place where Joseph stood; the place where the ass was
tethered; the "Milk Grotto," where Mary nursed her child;
and even the locality where twelve thousand of the infants
slain by the order of Herod were buried. But these of
course do not vie in sanctity with the spot where it is said
the Saviour of the world was born. That is called the
Chapel of the Nativity, and was evidently once a cave.
Believers in its authenticity maintain that it was at that
time used as a stable, and was situated below the little
caravansary, from which the Holy Family was excluded
because "there was no room for them in the inn." Its walls

are now of marble, and a silver star in the pavement marks
the place where the manger stood.

There is this to be said in favor of the genuineness of the
site of the Nativity: the tradition in regard to it is far
older than the time of Constantine and his mother, Helena.

Early in the second cen-
tury the place of Jesus'
birth was affirmed to have
been a cave close to the
village of Bethlehem. The
Empress Helena caused a
church to ·be erected
there, some portions of
which still exist. Hence,
it is the oldest existing
Christian sanctuary in the
world; and it is a touching
fact that the Crusader,
Baldwin I, when made King
of Jerusalem, refused to
wear a crown of gold in
the city where his Lord

WOMAN OF BETHLEHEM.

and Master had been crowned with thorns, and therefore
selected this church in Bethlehem, rather than Jerusalem,
for the place of his coronation.

Close by the Chapel of the Nativity, and covered by the
roof which canopies them both, is the tomb of Saint Jerome
and beside it we were shown the cavern in which that vener-
able father labored and prayed for more than thirty years.
Here he achieved his immortal work of translating the Scriptures into the Latin tongue, and here also he wrote no less
than one hundred and fifty epistles, sixteen theological
treatises, and thirteen volumes of commentaries. And
finally, here occurred the touching incident which has been

GROTTO OF THE NATIVITY.

immortalized by Domenichino, in his painting entitled " The Last Communion of Saint Jerome.'

From Bethlehem our route led on, a few miles farther, to Hebron, the earliest seat of civilization in. Palestine, and one of the oldest cities in the world. Here Abraham resided; here he received the three celestial visitors, and here his tomb

PILGRIMS AT BETHLEHEM.

is to this day. Hebron was also David's capital for the first seven years of his reign, till he transferred the seat of his sovereignty to Jerusalem. It is, accordingly, gratifying to find in a town of such antiquity some relics of the past whose genuineness cannot be questioned, although their age sur- passes that of all the other genuine memorials of Bible char- acters. To see these with safety, as soon as we arrived in Hebron, we made arrangements with the chief of the com- munity, Sheik Hamza. He did not look like one possess- ing much authority. In one hand he held a pipe to solace his old age, while with the other he grasped a knotty stick, which served him in turn as a scèptre and an instrument of discipline. The favor of this Sheik is, nevertheless, quite essential, for the Arabs of the place are noted for their hatred of all unbelievers; and the old spirit of intolerance, which once prevailed throughout the whole of Palestine and

SHEIK HAMZA.

made the entrance of a Christian to the Mosque of Omar an impossibility, still burns in Hebron bosoms undiminished by the lapse of years.

Properly protected, however, we made our way without difficulty to one of Hebron's famous relics,— its ancient reservoir of water, constructed of huge blocks of carefully hewn stone. Accustomed, as we were, to find fictitious names and dates assigned

to almost everything in Palestine, it startled us to learn that this reservoir was probably built in the time of David, three thousand years ago. Such, at all events, is the opinion of most archæologists; for cisterns like this and the celebrated "Pools of Solomon" were absolutely essential even in earliest times in a land like Palestine. Built with such solidity, they could last for centuries, and repairs, when needed, could be easily made without disturbing the original site. The Bible states that David put to death within this town the murderers of the son of Saul, and hung their lifeless bodies by the Pool of Hebron. It may, therefore, be surmised that, since no trace of other ruined reservoirs has been discovered anywhere in this vicinity, this is the identical basin described.

But of far greater interest than this Pool of Hebron is an object now enclosed by the massive walls of a Moslem mosque. The Christian traveler may survey their exterior at a respectful distance, but if he places the slightest value on his life, he should not try to enter the enclosure. Beneath the mosque, which these high battlements surround, there is a cave. It is the cavern of Machpelah, which Abraham, on the death of his wife Sarah, purchased as a family burial-place, nearly four thousand years ago. Here he himself was also buried; and, later on, within this cave were laid

POOL OF HEBRON.

to rest Isaac and Jacob, with their wives,—Jacob's body having, at the patriarch's request, been brought from Egypt to be placed here by the side of his wife, Leah. Moreover, since it was embalmed, after the manner of Egyptians, his features probably remain well-nigh intact to-day.

It is humiliating to admit that neither Jew nor Christian can to-day stand beside the tombs in which repose the founders of the Hebrew nation. But such is the fact; for the Mohammedans guard with jealous reverence the tomb of Abraham, for whom their name is "The Friend of God."

ABRAHAM'S OAK — HEBRON.

It is a singular coincidence that such a title should be given him by Moslems, for in the Epistle of St. James we read these words: "Abraham believed God, and it was imputed unto him for righteousness: and he was called the Friend of God." Of course, no illustrations of the tombs themselves can be obtained so long as such restrictions exist; but one may view at least the entrance to the patriarch's sepulchre, guarded by solid masonry and iron bars. By a special firman from Constantinople, in 1862, the Prince of Wales was admitted here, attended by Dean Stanley. In 1866, a similar favor was accorded to the Marquis of Bute; and three years after to the Crown Prince of Prussia, the late Emperor Frederick. One can imagine, therefore, what chance there is for ordinary tourists to enter.

According to the accounts of those who came here with these princely visitors, the tombs of Abraham, Sarah, Jacob, and Leah are in separate apartments lined with marble and approached through silver gates. The place of honor, in the

THE BANISHMENT OF HAGAR.

centre, is occupied by the tomb of Isaac. Between the
tombs of Abraham and Isaac is a circular opening; and it
appears probable that the structures which are seen are
merely modern cenotaphs, the actual sepulchres being in a
subterranean cavern at a still lower depth. The floor of the
enclosure is covered to some depth with pieces of paper,
which represent the accumulations of centuries. They are
written petitions to Abraham, which pious Moslems have
dropped through an aperture above.

"Is this the real cave of Machpelah?" we inquired.
"Can this be the actual tomb which Abraham acquired forty
centuries ago, with all the formality and care revealed in the
description given of that bargain in the Book of Genesis?"

It seems at first incredible; but there are many
arguments in favor of its
genuineness. In the first
place, a tomb like this,
cut from the solid rock,
would (if not purposely
destroyed) endure as long
as the surrounding hills.
Again, since Abraham
was a distinguished man,
and a powerful leader at
the time of his death, it
was at once revered as an
especially sacred burial-
place, the sanctity of

CAVE OF MACHPELAH.

which increased as time went by. Neither Jews nor Christians, Arabs nor Crusaders, have ever shown the slightest
disposition to disturb the graves of those illustrious dead.
In fact, the evidence is so remarkably complete that few, if
any, are disposed to question it. Undoubtedly, the time

will come when the exclusion practiced by the Moslems will be overruled, and this extraordinary relic of antiquity will be thrown open to Christian eyes and thoroughly explored. But even now, the fact that Hebron holds the cavern of Machpelah, in which four thousand years ago were

buried the great patriarchs of the Hebrew race, gives to this region of Judæa a unique importance and undying fame.

Our visit to Hebron naturally recalled to us that lovely painting in the Dresden Gallery, portraying Hagar driven from the house of Abraham, and going forth with her child Ishmael to live and die in exile. How little did the patriarch think, when he reluctantly con- sented to that sad expulsion, that the descendants of the outcast Hagar would for a thousand years exclude the offspring of her rival

WOMAN AND CHILD — HEBRON.

Sarah from all access to his tomb! Yet so it is. The rock- hewn sepulchres of Abraham and Isaac have been for cen- turies protected by the sons of Ishmael.

Filled with the memories awakened by the patriarchs' graves, on our return to Jerusalem we visited one of its most impressive features. It is an ancient wall, consisting largely of huge blocks of stone, which once formed part of the old Hebrew temple. This to the Jews is by far the most sacred portion of the city. What matters it to them that Christian sects wrangle or worship round the Holy Sepulchre, or that Mohammedans kneel in prayer within the Mosque of Omar? They know that these colossal fragments of the time of Solo- mon antedate by a thousand years even the oldest of all such

memorials. Here, every Friday, century after century, the
wretched exiles from Mount Zion have come to kiss or bathe
with tears these relics of their former glory. Now they are
free to do so; but in past ages they have paid enormous sums
to their oppressors for this miserable privilege.

It is a most pathetic instance of a nation's grief. No one
who has a particle of sympathy with human sorrow can gaze
upon that sight without emo-
tion. For, while some read
aloud from the Old Testa-
ment words which describe the
splendor of the Hebrew mon-
archy, others moan and sob,
and beat their trembling hands
against the wall. Their grief
is evidently genuine, for I saw
tears on many a cheek, especially when such plaintive passages from Holy Writ as these
were read: "How hath the
Lord cast down from heaven
to earth the beauty of Israel!
How is the gold become dim
and the most fine gold changed!

JEWS' WAILING PLACE.

Our holy and our beautiful house, wherein our fathers
praised Thee, is burned up with fire. We are become a scorn
and a derision to our neighbors. Oh, Lord! behold, we are
Thy people. Remember not our iniquity forever. Oh! let
Thy tender mercies speedily redeem us! We are brought
very low."

What wonder that they mourn? For nineteen dreary centuries their history has been one almost uninterrupted trag-
edy. Scattered throughout the world, scorned of all nations,
they have been forced to suffer every form of persecution

which men have been sufficiently cruel and ingenious to
invent. Words fail to depict their sufferings. To torture, rob and exile them, the despotism of a hundred kings
has been exhausted. They have been bought and sold as
slaves. The plague which devastated Europe
in the Middle Ages was ascribed to them, with
horrible results. In France, throughout whole

provinces, every Jew was burned.
In Germany, too, their history for
centuries is a hideous chronicle of
human cruelty. Even in England
their persecution, sketched in outline
by Sir Walter Scott in *Ivanhoe*, is
nothing to the lurid picture which he
might have drawn.

As for Spain, no land in the world
has equaled this, the birthplace of
the Inquisition, in wreaking cruel
wrath on the unoffending Jew.
Many were here buried alive. In
one year, in Seville alone, two

JEWISH LADY AND MAID.

hundred and eighty are said to have perished in the flames.
Hebrews themselves consider their terrible expulsion from
Spain a misfortune equaled only by the ruin of their
Temple. We shudder at the brutal policy of Russia
toward the Jews to-day, but let us not forget that all
other Christian nations, except free America, have acted
in a similar way when they had reached Russia's present
stage of civilization. In the thirteenth century, all Jews
were banished from Great Britain and their property was
seized. In 1390 they were expelled from France; and
in 1492, the very year which witnessed the discovery of
America by Columbus, they were cast forth from Spain,
where they had lived protected by the Moors for six hundred

JEWISH PLACE OF LAMENTATION.

years, to wander through the world as hated exiles, and frequently to perish of starvation or by the slower agony of the
slave-whip.   If received at all in many Christian cities, they
were hived in certain limited districts, like the Ghetto at
Rome.   Moreover, by a refinement of torture, Jewish children under fourteen years of age were taken from their par-
ents, and retained in Spain and Portugal to be brought up as
Christians, so that, in their madness, Hebrew mothers would
sometimes murder their own offspring and then commit sui-
cide.   And why was all this misery in-
flicted on the Hebrew race?   Because the
Jews were said to have crucified Jesus.
But as a matter of fact the Jews did not
crucify Jesus.   It was the Romans who
scourged Him, put the crown of thorns
upon His brow, and finally nailed Him to
the cross.   True, the Jews solicited His
death.   But how many of them?   Only a
priestly sect in Jerusalem.   Is it fair to
condemn an entire people for the sins of a
few, and above all to persecute their
innocent descendants after hundreds of
years have come and gone?   That
would be a dangerous precedent to
establish!   According to that, we ought
to persecute the Greeks for causing
Socrates to drink the hemlock; the
Italians, because so many martyrs were
thrown to the lions in the Roman Colos-
seum; the Florentines for burning Savona-

ZION GATE, JERUSALEM.

rola; the English for the flames of Smithfield; the Spaniards
for the horrors of the Inquisition.

The Jews are not the only people who have rejected and
put to death their teachers and reformers.   Such conduct is

as old as history. In any case, what right have certain
nations (themselves not without sin) to act as executioners?
"Vengeance is mine, I will repay, saith the Lord."

Does it seem credible, therefore, in view of the fact that
Christian baptism has usually offered to the Jew an avenue
of escape from all these
horrors, that after nine-
teen hundred years of such
calamitous persecution,
one genuine Hebrew can
be left who has not ex-
changed his faith for the
religion of his tyrants?
Even in Russia, now, a
Jew may rid himself of
many restrictions by be-
coming a Christian. Here,
indeed, is the marvel of
it all,—the miracle of history,—that in direct op-
position to all motives of self-interest, the Jews not only
have remained, but still remain, sublimely loyal to their
fathers' faith. Nothing has shaken or divided them. They
have survived the empires which sought to destroy them.
Without a country, without a common, living language, and
without one political bond of union, they nevertheless exist
to-day a perfectly distinct and indestructible race, exulting
in their glorious past!

A MERCHANT.

And what a past is theirs! We need not dwell upon the
fact that they have given to mankind the Bible; that the
sublimest of religious prophecies, and the most eloquent of
sacred songs, were written by the Jews. We need not even
elaborate the startling truth that from Judæa have come
forth the three religions which so influence the race—Juda-

ism, Christianity, and Islamism. Let all that for a moment
go, while we consider later history. Through the darkness
of the Middle Ages, when most of Europe lay in densest
ignorance, the Jews still held aloft the torch of learning.
They (with the Moors) were then the scholars of the world.
From their ranks came the ablest financiers, the profoundest
philosophers, and the most remarkable physicians. And even
now, despite their persecution, the influence of their race is
still paramount in Jerusalem.

A short time ago a band of wretched Jewish refugees from
Russia landed on the Syrian coast. They were well-nigh
starving, and tottering from weakness. Babes were dying at
their mothers' breasts. They were rescued by means of the
Hebrew colonial fund, and finally proceeded toward the
shrine of their race
—Jerusalem.

Before them rose
the magnificent
Russian church
built on the Mount
of Olives, perhaps
upon the very place
where Jesus uttered
the words: "What-
soever ye would
that men should do
to you, do ye
even so to them."
Imagine those Jew-

RUSSIAN CHURCH — OLIVET.

ish exiles, to whom the very name, "Russia," was synony-
mous with torture, looking on that gilded shrine and
asking: "Who are the people worshiping in that church,—
Jews?"—and receiving the answer: "No, Russians, worshiping a Jew!" "Who are the thousands praying in the

church of the Holy Sepulchre,—Jews?" "No, Christians, worshiping Jesus of Nazareth!" "Who are the hundreds kneeling in the Mosque of Omar,—Jews?" "No, Moslems, praying there because it is hallowed by the memory of Hebrew patriarchs."

GAMBETTA.

Truly, the Jew, persecuted though he be, may smile in triumph; for wherever he looks about him in Palestine, from the undoubted tomb of Abraham to the reputed sepulchre of Jesus, he sees the followers of Christ and Mohammed all zealously guarding memorials of his own race. And what must be his secret pride, when he reflects that every word of the Christian Bible was written by Jews, that the Moslem Bible, the Koran, is founded on the Jewish faith, and that the entire Christian world worships Jesus of Nazareth as divine, and a vast proportion of it also reverences a Jewish woman as the Mother of the Son of God!

In a place so thronged with classic and religious memories as Palestine, even a man who has no Hebrew blood in his veins may indulge in a dream regarding the future of this extraordinary people. Suppose a final solution of the "Eastern Question." Suppose the nations of the earth to be assembled in council, as they were in Berlin a few years ago. Suppose the miserably governed realm of the Sultan to be diminished in size. Imagine some portions of it to be governed by various European powers, as Egypt is governed by England at the present time. Conceive that those Christian nations, moved by magnanimity, should say to this race which they, or their ancestors, have persecuted so long: "Take again the land of your forefathers. We guarantee you its independence and integrity. It is the least that we can do

for you after all these centuries of misery. All of you will
not wish to go thither, but many will. At present Palestine
supports only six hundred thousand people, but, with proper
cultivation it can easily maintain two and a half millions.
You are a people without a country; there is a country without a people. Be united. Fulfil the dreams of your old poets
and patriarchs. Go back,—go back to the land of Abraham.''

But were this dream realized, could the Jews become a
nation? They certainly have produced great statesmen.
Who does not recollect Gambetta, that indefatigable hero of
the French nation after its terrible defeat by Germany? He
was a Jew. So was Count Von Arnim, the German diplo-
mat. So was Lasker, the liberal leader of the Prussian parliament, the only man in that assembly whom Bismarck really
feared. Jews were some years ago the Mayors of the principal cities of England, including Lon-
don; while, in less than a century
after their political disabilities had
been removed in England, the
Premier of the Queen's domin-
ions, the virtual sovereign of
the British empire, was the
Hebrew, Benjamin Disraeli, Earl
of Beaconsfield. You recollect
that when he was taunted once
in Parliament with being a Jew,
he rose and answered: ''Yes, I
am a Jew, but let me remind
the honorable gentleman that,

DISRAELI.

when his ancestors were savages on the banks of the Thames,
mine were princes in Solomon's temple!''

What have they done in modern literature?

The most eloquent orator and the most brilliant writer
in Spain, Emilio Castelar, is a Hebrew.

The majority of the professorial chairs in Germany are occupied by Jews. Two-thirds of the journalism of Europe to-day is said to be controlled by Hebrews. Out of three hundred and seventy authors in the Austrian Empire, two hundred and twenty-five are Jews. The poet Heine was of Hebrew descent; so was the German novelist, Auerbach. And the Hebrew Spinoza was the father of modern philosophy.

In art and music it is the same. Once give the Jew a chance, and he springs into the front rank of his competitors; the splendid genius of the race leaping into flame like a row of lights, when the torch is passed along the line. Thus Munkacsy, the Hungarian painter, was a Hebrew. So were the famous actresses Rachel and Janauschek. So is that woman of surpassing histrionic genius, Sarah Bernhardt. It is impossible to enumerate all the musicians found among the

CASTELAR.

Jews, but we may mention Moscheles, Wieniawski, Joachim, and Rubenstein, as well as the mighty composers, Halévy, Rossini, Meyerbeer and Mendelssohn.

How is it in finance?

Here they are unrivaled. The Jews are the bankers of the world. The banking business of the Austrian empire is managed by Hebrews, who could foreclose and ruin many of the nobles who in society treat them with disdain. The principal banker of Prussia is the Hebrew, Bleichröder; while the Jewish house of the Rothschilds controls the diplomacy of empires.

The Jews, we know, are often reproached with being merely financiers, and with doing little or nothing in industrial or pastoral pursuits. But why is this? Because until recently everywhere, and even now in certain portions of the world, the Jews have not been allowed to own a foot of soil, or to enter any manufacturing guilds.

Accordingly, being restricted to finance, they have taken their revenge by managing the money commerce of the world.

Again, the Jews are often blamed because of their fondness for gems. But for centuries they were compelled to carry their wealth in that portable and easily secreted form, since, whenever suspected of having property, they usually escaped having their teeth

SIR MOSES MONTEFIORE.

pulled, or their nails drawn out by the roots, only by yielding it up to their persecutors.

We all dislike the petty avarice of small Jewish traders, but let us in charity remember that they are but exhibiting the traits that centuries of persecution have ground into them.

"Our deeds still travel with us from afar,
And what we have been makes us what we are."

BARON HIRSCH.

The death of that grand benefactor of his race, Sir Moses Montefiore, reminded us of another characteristic of the Jews,—their philanthropy. He was so well known for his benevolence, that on the one hundredth anniversary of his birth (in 1884), he received the homage of the civilized world; and he it was who first proposed the scheme of rescuing his persecuted brethren and forming them into well managed colonies in various countries. This scheme was ably seconded by his successor in benevolence, the late Baron Hirsch, whose charity was on a scale unprecedented in the

annals of philanthropy, for he gave fifteen million dollars for
the relief of his outcast co-religionists! Russian tyranny,
therefore, colossal though it was, encountered Jewish charity
more colossal still. The first exemplified the record of
a down-trodden race; the second stood for justice and hu-
mane treatment in the years to come. We cannot doubt
which of these forces will finally overcome the other, under

the influence of Him who in His
earthly life was born of a Jewish
mother and was to all intents and
purposes a Jew. Yet, notwithstand-
ing these facts, perhaps some reader
of these words may say: "It is all
true, but—we do not like the Jew!"
But shall we not take a broader and
kindlier view than that? Rising
above individual likes and dislikes,
let us ask ourselves if it is, or ever
has been, consistent for Christian
nations to oppress and despise the people who gave to them
their patriarchs, their prophets, their Bible, their religion and
their Saviour. Nearly nineteen centuries have come and
gone since Jesus died upon the cross. Surely it is time for
His teachings of charity and the brotherhood of man to prevail among his followers. For—

> " New occasions teach new duties;
>   Time makes ancient good uncouth;
>   They must upward still, and onward,
>   Who would keep abreast of Truth:
>   Lo, before us gleam her camp-fires!
>   We ourselves must Pilgrims be,
>   Launch our Mayflower, and steer boldly
>   Through the desperate winter sea:
>   Nor attempt the Future's portal
>   With the Past's blood-rusted key."

LECTURE I

———

NORWÄY

———

THE first lecture of the series Mr. John L. Stoddard
devotes to NORWAY, and he furnishes a strik-
ingly realistic portrayal of this land of the Sagas and
Vikings. The 128 illustrations—reproductions of
photographs made for Mr. Stoddard on the spot—are
worthy accompaniments of the sparkling text.

As we read it we fancy ourselves sailing up the
picturesque fjords and whirling along the mountain-
roads—on, onward from Christiania, through scenery
varied by cascades and precipices—on till we reach
the North Cape, and view, just above the waves,

THE MIDNIGHT SUN

———

This first lecture will be sent, post-paid, on receipt
of the introductory price charged for the second lecture.

JOHN L. STODDARD'S LECTURES

Illustrated and Embellished with Views of the World's Famous Places and People, being the identical discourses delivered during the past eighteen years under the title of THE STODDARD LECTURES.

VOL. I NOW READY

VOLUME I CONTAINS MR. STODDARD'S LECTURES ON

NORWAY, SWITZERLAND, ATHENS-VENICE

Over 360 Beautiful Reproductions of Photographs

Sold only by subscription. To be completed in Ten Octavo Volumes.

BELFORD, MIDDLEBROOK & CO.
PUBLISHERS

CHICAGO, ILL.

JOHN L. STODDARD'S LECTURES

WHAT IS THOUGHT OF THE FIRST VOLUME

"The frequent use of anecdotes gives a life to Mr. Stoddard's pages that they would otherwise lack. The illustrations are the next best thing to visiting the places themselves. If Mr. Stoddard never does anything more, these ten volumes will be a worthy monument of his life work."—*The Chicago Tribune.*

"I do not remember that I have ever seen as handsome a book. * * It is simply superb. The illustrations are unexcelled, and the text is limpid and pleasant and easy, and takes me back again to the delightful hours when I sat and heard it recited, and looked upon the pictures in larger, but not more beautiful form. Stoddard is an ideal lecturer, and his work is an ideal work."—*James Charlton, General Passenger Agent Chicago & Alton Railroad.*

"During the past twenty years Mr. Stoddard's lectures have done more to educate the American public in literature and the arts, and bring before them the great world and its people, their histories and customs, than any other one hundred persons have accomplished. * * * are so beautifully described and so magnificently illustrated that it does not seem possible to wait for Vol. II."—*New Haven Union.*

"The lectures are certainly very interesting indeed, and I believe the book as it stands is the handsomest thing I have ever seen in the shape of a book, the illustrations, paper, and binding being A No. 1."—*Chas. S. Fee, General Passenger Agent Northern Pacific Ry.*

"To attend a course of lectures by Mr. Stoddard is a liberal education in itself, and almost as good as a pleasure trip around the world. To have those lectures in one's library, published in such artistic form and with illustrations which represent the very highest standard of art, is indeed a boon."—*Albany Times-Union.*

BELFORD, MIDDLEBROOK & CO.

PUBLISHERS

CHICAGO, ILL,

LECTURE III

JERUSALEM

M R. JOHN L. STODDARD devotes the third lecture of the series to JERUSALEM and its environs, conducting us to spots familiar by name to all Bible-readers, and recounting, in his inimitable way, the religious and historical associations of each. Under the magic of his words, time and space are as naught; we stand where Jesus stood, we gaze upon the same scenes that the Disciples knew. What a flood of ideas overwhelms us! We linger on the Mount of Olives, we look wistfully upon a landscape changed and darkened by the vicissitudes of nineteen centuries. An alien race now dwells where Christianity had its lowly birth, but no alien faith can bar its march. It has gone forth to the uttermost ends of the earth, and, as tokens of its power, we see to-day gorgeous shrines and churches erected here by nations beyond the sea.

120 ILLUSTRATIONS

all of them reproduced from special photographs, adorn the text and heighten the reader's interest.

Lecture III will be sent, postpaid, at the same low introductory price asked for ATHENS and VENICE.

SWITZERLAND

Our next tour in Mr. John L. Stoddard's agreeable company will be to a land where Nature seems to have been most prodigal of scenic beauty and commanding grandeur. Ice-sheeted mountains zigzag the horizon, darkling crevasses beset our way, and from their inaccessible lairs creep forth those frozen rivers that are the wonder of scientists and the delight of sightseers. Mr. Stoddard very considerately refrains from taking us into actual dangers, but he tells enough of mountain-climbing in the Swiss Alps to show the perils braved. Besides the glaciers and the picturesque villages that cling to the mountain-side in defiance of the avalanches, there are the lakes and waterfalls to interest us. We stand in Chillon's historic dungeon, where Bonnivard was chained, we pause amid scenes familiar to Voltaire, Rousseau, Gibbon, and Byron, and we feel a deeper thrill at history's lessons when we realize what this sturdy little republic has accomplished.

121 Illustrations,

exquisite reproductions of Mr. Stoddard's specially prepared photographs and others, place this lecture on the same artistic level with the three preceding ones—NORWAY, ATHENS-VENICE, and JERUSALEM, and it will be sent, postpaid, at the same special price.